Let's Start! ICT

Finding Facts

Anne Rooney

QED Publishing

Copyright © QED Publishing 2005

First published in the UK in 2005 by
QED Publishing
A Quarto Group company
226 City Road
London EC1V 2TT

www.qed-publishing.co.uk

A Catalogue record for this book is available from
the British Library.

ISBN 1 84538 189 0

Written by Anne Rooney
Designed by Jacqueline Palmer
Editor Louisa Somerville
Consultant Philip Stubbs
Illustrator John Haslam
Illustrations page 29 Luki Sumner-Rooney
Photographer Ray Moller
Models provided by Scallywags

Publisher Steve Evans
Creative Director Louise Morley
Editorial Manager Jean Coppendale

Printed and bound in China

Words in bold **like this** are explained in the Glossary on page 30.

Contents

About Finding Facts

You see and hear all kinds of **information** every day. Some of it you find for yourself – you read a book, ask a question or watch TV. But lots of it is just around you, trying to make you notice it!

Spotting information

What information can you see around you right now? For a start, there's this book! But you can probably see posters, wall displays, labels and writing.

Pictures, such as signs, maps, paintings and cartoons, give us information.

Words people say give information, too. We talk to each other and listen to CDs, radio and television.

Other sounds give information – the school bell, a fire alarm and a police car siren all tell us something.

On the computer

A computer shows you information in words, pictures and sounds.

What does it mean?

Information has all sorts of messages. It can warn us, teach us or make us laugh.

Time to get up

What's it telling you?

Some information tells you useful things – like the way out of the supermarket, or which toilet is for boys and which for girls, how to play a game or when it's safe to cross the road.

PLEASE
DO NOT
FEED

How do we know?

If you see a sign showing a bicycle crossed out, you can guess it means 'no cycling'. That is because you can 'read' the message in the picture.

New Film
Alien

Don't miss it

Advertisements try to get you to spend money.

Come to the
CIRCUS
1-5 May

at Queen's Park

Yum-Yum
CHOCOBAR

IT'S
YUMMY!

7

Storing information

You can use the computer to store your work – and all kinds of other information, too.

Doing it yourself

When you do your own work on the computer, you use the keyboard and the mouse to put in the words you want. You can use the mouse to draw pictures if you have a painting or drawing program.

When you've finished your work, you can print it out so that you have a copy on paper that you can show to other people.

You can also save your work onto a CD-ROM so that you can use it again later.

Do you want to save your work?

Yes No

click to choose

Making choices

Sometimes the computer needs to ask you a question. It appears on the screen. You can type your answer or choose one by clicking on a button.

Menus

The computer can also offer you choices by showing you a set of words or pictures called a **menu**.

Choose a picture to colour in.

click to choose

new document | open folder | save | print

Pictures

The computer uses **icons** – little pictures that stand for something. You've probably seen some of these icons and may already know what they mean.

Listen carefully!

Sometimes the computer speaks words. This is helpful if you can't read all the words on the screen.

All ears

Sounds can give you extra information, such as playing a tune or teaching you animal noises. That's something most books can't do!

Farmyard sounds

Mooo

click to choose

It might play the sound as soon as you open the screen, or there might be a button to click on to hear the sound.

Sounds for fun

Games often use sounds, such as the sound of cars in a racing game. Sounds can make the game much more exciting.

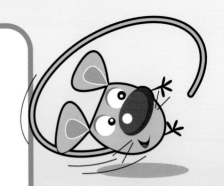

Brmm brmm

Screech

When computers use sounds, pictures, words and even moving cartoons or bits of film, it's called **multimedia**. You can use multimedia for fun or to find things out.

All about frogs

See frog photos

Hear frog sounds

Watch frog videos

Frogs lay eggs which are called frogspawn – when they hatch, they are called tadpoles.

Telling stories

You can read or listen to stories from books, or use the computer.

Talking books

A talking book on the computer tells a story using words, pictures and sounds. You can read the story yourself on the screen, or get the computer to read it to you.

This is the story of Waltrude the witch and Fin her cat...

click to hear story

Practise!

If you've got a talking book, try this:

Find a button to click on to make the computer read the words.

Move the mouse over a word.

She cast a spell.

Abracadabra

click to hear word

If the computer doesn't read it out, click on the word. Does it read now?

Coming to life

You can click buttons or move across parts of the picture to play sounds or see moving pictures.

Miaow

click to play

What happens next?

In a paper book, you turn over the pages to move on to the next bit of the story or check back to see what's happened before. With a talking book, you move to a new page using the mouse.

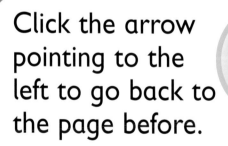

Follow the arrow

A talking book usually has arrow buttons on the screen for you to go forwards or backwards.

Click the arrow pointing to the right to move on to the next page.

Click the arrow pointing to the left to go back to the page before.

There might be arrows to go all the way back to the start:  or all the way to the end of the book:

You choose!

In a story book, you have to read the story from the beginning to the end, otherwise it doesn't make sense.

Some talking stories are like this, but some let you make choices.

What happens next in the story depends on what you choose.

This way That way

click to choose

Practise!

Try moving forwards and backwards through a talking book. Read the whole story.

Finding things out

There are lots of ways to find out things you want to know.

Using books

You can get some information from a person or from a book.

You could ask your teacher how big a tiger is, or you could look in a book about tigers.

Or you could watch TV programmes or videos about tigers.

If you want to find out a fact, it's usually quicker to ask or look in a book. You might watch a whole video and not find what you wanted.

Are we nearly there yet?

Many books give you help to find what you want. They have a **contents** page or an **index** so that you can look up what you want to know.

Ask a friend

For some kinds of information, the way to find out something is to ask someone. You ask the dinner lady what's for lunch, or you ask a friend what day their birthday is on.

It's all linked

You can look things up on the computer, too.

Links

CD-ROMs usually have an index and a contents list, just like a book. But they also have something books don't have – they have **links** between the pages so that you can jump around.

If a word is linked to another page, it usually has a line under it. It might also be in a different colour.

Just click on the linked word to make the new page come up on the screen.

Animals of the World

Kangaroos

Bears

Tigers

Elephants

Lions

Camels

click to find out more

More information

It can be much faster to look up information on a computer than in a book. If a book says 'elephants (see page 10)', you have to turn to that page for the information you need.

On the computer, the word 'elephants' is linked to the other page. Just click on it to see all about elephants.

Elephants

Elephants come from India and Africa.

Practise!

If you've got a CD-ROM, follow five links and see where you get to. Can you get back to where you started?

Moving around

If you follow lots of links, you might get lost! Luckily, books on CD-ROM have buttons to help you find your way around.

Going back

When you follow a link, you can easily get back to where you were before.

Look for an arrow with the word 'Back' pointing to the left. This will take you back to the last page you looked at.

Back

You might be on a page about rockets. Then you click on a link to astronauts. To get back to rockets again, just click the Back button.

Rockets

Rockets take astronauts into space.

Fire comes out of the engine at the back of the rocket as it takes off.

Back

go back to the last page that you looked at

Back

Astronauts

An astronaut wears a special suit and an air tank to work in space.

go back one page

go back to the beginning

go to the end

go forward one page

Remember that there are other arrows on the page, too. They take you forward or back one page, or right to the beginning or end of the topic.

More moving!

You won't always want to move through the CD-ROM in order. You can move around in other ways, too.

Going home

Sometimes, there's a button to go right back to the beginning. It often has a picture of a house because the first page is called the 'home' page.

Contents

Index

What else is there?

There is usually a button to go to the index or contents page, or for both.

The index or contents list of a CD-ROM doesn't have page numbers, like in a paper book. Instead, it has links.

The contents shows a list of what's on the CD-ROM.

CONTENTS

Look after your pet:

 Cat

 Dog

 Fish

 Rabbit

click to find out more

Rabbits

A rabbit needs a hutch and somewhere to run around. It also needs clean water and fresh food each day.

The index lists lots of words you may want to look for on the CD-ROM, to help you find a topic.

INDEX

<u>cat</u>	<u>kitten</u>
<u>dog</u>	<u>leads</u>
<u>fish</u> <u>food</u>	<u>puppy</u>
<u>green</u> <u>food</u>	<u>rabbit</u>
<u>hay</u>	<u>tank</u>
<u>hutch</u>	<u>weed</u>

click to find topic

Keep searching

If you can't find what you want in the index or contents, you can ask the computer to look for it.

Find or search

Many CD-ROMs have a **Search** button. This lets you look for one or more words.

Click the Search button to see a box where you can type in the word you want to look for.

Search  Type word here

click here to search

24

Using keywords

The word you search for is called a **keyword**. Choosing the right keyword takes a bit of practise.

Imagine you have a CD-ROM about animals and you want to find out about baby cats. If you can't find a link from the cats page, you could search for 'baby'.

baby

But the computer doesn't know you want to find out about baby cats. It will suggest lots of other baby animals, as well as cats.

Searching for 'kitten' or 'baby cat' will take you straight to what you need.

kitten

25

Over to you

Now it's time to do some work of your own. You'll need a CD-ROM that has a contents list or index, and links between the pages.

Treasure hunt!

Make a treasure hunt for words. Then ask a friend to find the treasure.

1. Choose a linked word from the contents list. Write it down on paper.

2. Click on the link to open the linked page.

3. On the page that opens, pick another link.

4. Again, write down a linked word, then click on it.

5. Do this until you've followed at least three links.

6. Write a clue for your friend, to help them to click on the first linked word you wrote down.

For example, if you chose 'turtles', your clue might be:

It's green or brown, lives in the water and has a shell.

Make sure only one topic on the page fits your clue.

Turtles

Turtles are like <u>tortoises</u> but they live in the <u>water</u>.

Water

Most of the Earth is covered in water. We find it in the <u>sea</u>, in <u>rivers</u> and even in <u>clouds</u>.

Rivers

Rivers are used for <u>transport</u>. In some countries they are more important than <u>roads</u>.

7. Think of a clue for each of your other links, right through to the final answer.

8. Tell your friend to open the contents page of the CD-ROM. Give them the clues and see how they do!

Make a talking book

Make your own **talking book** – without using the computer!

You'll need six pieces of paper.

1. Draw six pictures to make a story or copy the pictures on the next page. Write a line of words above each picture.

2. On each page, draw arrows to go forwards and backwards, back to the beginning and right to the end.

3. Work out what will happen on each page. Then draw a star where someone could click to see or hear something.

Imagine, if your talking book was on the computer, what could it do? If someone clicked on an animal or person, would it make a noise? Or would it do an action?

1. Frank the cat fell asleep in the garden.

2. A bird flew by.

3. The bird landed near Frank.

4. Frank pounced on the bird.

5. The bird pecked Frank on the head.

6. Lucy put a plaster on Frank.

4. Ask a friend to use your book – you have to pretend to be the computer!

If your friend points at an arrow, give them the right page.

If they point at a sentence, read it out.

If they point at a star, do the action or sound!

Glossary

contents   List of main topics covered in a book or CD-ROM.

icon   Small picture that stands for something.

index   List of subject words that appear in a book or CD-ROM.

information   Facts about something.

keyword   Word you use to carry out a search on a CD-ROM.

link   One or more words or objects that, if you click on them, will open a new page on a CD-ROM or website.

menu   List of things you can choose from on the computer.

multimedia   Information on the computer that uses a mixture of words, pictures, sounds and sometimes movies.

search   Tool used to find out about a topic.

talking book   Story book on the computer that will read words out to you.

Index

Grown-up zone

Finding Facts
and the National Curriculum

The work in this book will help children to cover the following parts of the National Curriculum ICT scheme of work: most of unit 1c, unit 2c.

It can be tied in with work on any other area of the curriculum in which the children use the computer or books to research a topic and find out information.

Provide suitable talking stories and books or encyclopedias on CD-ROM for children to work with. Make sure the language is approriate for their age and that there are clear contents, navigation aids and search facilities that children will be able to use. Give children precise instructions so that they research topics that have links to other useful, related material. Help them to identify and try out different keywords, and discuss the results of their searches.

Encourage children to work together and discuss how to find information using a combination of contents or index, following links and using search terms. Help them to talk about which keywords were most successful and why they think this might be.

Children should be encouraged to review, evaluate and improve their own work at all stages.